Naugh Children

by Alison Hawes

Contents

PEARSON
Longman

No! said Mo

"Time for school," said Miss Bun.
"Time for school. Time for fun!"

"No!" said Mo. "I won't go!"

"Time for music," said Miss Bun.
"Time for music. Time for fun!"

"No!" said Mo. "I won't go!"

"Time for PE," said Miss Bun.
"Time for PE. Time for fun!"

"No!" said Mo. "I won't go!"

"Time for play," said Miss Bun.
"Time for play. Time for fun!"

"No!" said Mo. "I won't go!"

"Time to go home," said Mo's Mum.

"No!" said Mo. "I won't come!"

Don't Forget!

Mum said, "Can you go to the chip shop?"
"Yes!" we said.

"Can you get three fish and a big bag of chips?"
"Yes!" we said.

"Three fish and a *big* bag of chips," said Mum.
"Now don't forget!"

14

"We will not forget!" we said.

We went in the chip shop.
We did not forget.
We got three fish and a **big** bag
of chips.

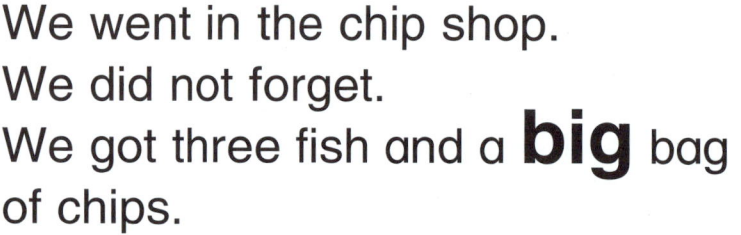

We had one chip.
Then we had two chips.

Then we had three chips.
And then we had *lots* of chips!

We gave the fish and chips to Mum.

"This is a *little* bag of chips," she said.
"Did you forget to get a big bag?"

"Yes," we said.

No Tapping!

Dad and I went to the zoo.
My little brother came with us.

We looked at the frogs.
My little brother tapped on the glass.

"No tapping!" said Dad.
"Look. It says: 'Do not tap on the glass'!"

"The frogs don't like it," I said.

Then we went to see the monkeys.
My little brother tapped on the glass.

"*No* tapping!" said Dad.
"The monkeys don't like it."

We looked at the fish next.
My little brother tapped on the glass.

Dad was cross.
"I said NO tapping!" he said.
"The fish don't like it!"

Then we had a look at the lions.
My little brother tapped on the glass.

The lion **roared!**
It made my brother jump.

He did not tap on the glass again!